This book belong
Alondra

This book is dedicated to my children - Mikey, Kobe, and Jojo.

By Mary Nhin

Illustrated By
Yuliia Zolotova

Muhammad Ali

I grew up in the United States in the early twentieth century. It was a hard time for many people including me.

I struggled in school because I had dyslexia, which meant that I had difficulties with reading and writing. There wasn't much support for me, so I wasn't able to excel in my studies.

I, also, struggled outside of school because I am African American, and there was a lot of racism in America.

Because of this, I felt down a lot of the time until I found my passion, boxing.

I took up boxing when I was twelve years old. I hadn't even heard of it until one day my bicycle was stolen. The police officer told me that if I wanted to fight the thief to get my bike back, I'd better learn how to box!

It's a lack of faith that makes people afraid of meeting challenges, and I believe in myself.

I went home and watched an amateur boxing match on the television for the first time. I was mesmerized. It was so exciting, and I knew I had to try it for myself.

I began training and I never looked back. I learned to fight and won a gold medal at the summer Olympics in Rome.

By age eighteen, I had become a professional boxer!

I was inspired by the WWF, World Wrestling Federation, wrestlers I'd seen. I tried acting tough and scary to my competitors so that people would think I was fun to watch. Not everybody liked my style, but it certainly made me a character people wanted to watch.

He who is not courageous enough to take risks will accomplish nothing in life.

I became a heavyweight champion at just 22 years old. I proved that although I faced a lot of challenges growing up, I became a success.

Only a man who knows what it is like to be defeated can reach down to the bottom of his soul and come up with the extra ounce of power it takes to win when the match is even.

Timeline

1960 – Muhammad wins a gold medal at the
         Olympics in Rome

1964 – Muhammad becomes the youngest boxer
         to defeat the reigning heavyweight champion

1997 – Muhammad is awarded the BET
         Humanitarian Award

2009 – Muhammad receives the NAACP
         President's Award

minimovers.tv

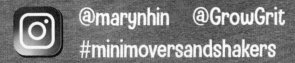 @marynhin   @GrowGrit
#minimoversandshakers

 Mary Nhin   Ninja Life Hacks

 Ninja Life Hacks

 @marynhin

Made in the USA
Middletown, DE
22 May 2023